BLACKSHAW MOOR
POLISH CAMP
1946 -1964

Zosia and Jurek Biegus

Printed by 4edge Ltd., Hockley, Essex
First printing August 2015

ISBN 978-0-992887957

Acknowledgments

Zbyszek Hryciuk; for sharing his personal experience of living in the camp
and contributing many of the photographs illustrating this publication.

Angela Rhead; for reading through the draft and suggesting changes to make
it more accessible to readers unfamiliar with the post war history of the Polish
community in the UK.

Blackshaw Moor

Situated in the Staffordshire Moorlands, on the southern edge of the Peak District and overlooking the impressive rocky outcrops of the Roaches, Blackshaw Moor is not only a walkers' paradise offering magnificent views across the moors but for those interested in the aftermath of WW2, this area has a story of its own.

"There is not much left now of Little Poland on Blackshaw Moor. Not much left, that is, of the ugly collection of Nissen huts which used to spoil the view of the Staffordshire Moorlands for passing motorists. Those huts always had a haunting quality for me, providing a nagging reminder of those grimmest camps of all time in Central Europe in The War, where so many Polish and Jewish people died, with great dignity and bravery."

(From an article written by John Abberley of BBC Radio Stoke on Trent for "The Spark" a local publication.)

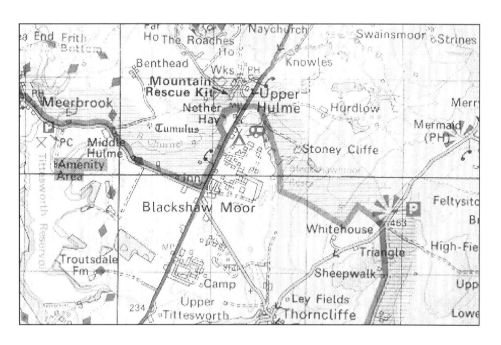

The War and its aftermath

Following the defeat of the Polish army by the joint forces of Hitler's Germany and Stalin's USSR in the September Campaign of 1939, an order went out for Polish soldiers to make their way, as best they could, to France where a Polish Government in Exile was formed under the premiership of Gen. Sikorski and a Polish army was being assembled to continue fighting alongside Poland's allies – Britain and France. Those who did not make it across Italy to France headed for Syria where they were formed into the Carpathian Rifle Brigade, which later fought at Tobruk. The forces that formed in France participated in the abortive Narvik campaign and, following the defeat of France in 1940, evacuated to Britain.

In the meantime Hitler's ally, Stalin, was consolidating his hold on the part of Poland the Soviet Union had annexed under the Ribbentrop – Molotov pact, by deporting to Siberia anyone thought likely to resist the annexation. By the time Hitler broke the pact with the Soviet Union and attacked it on the 22nd June 1941, close to a million Poles had been deported. However, Germany's attack on the Soviet Union brought the Soviets into the Allied camp with Britain and, more awkwardly Poland. Consequently, Stalin declared a so called "amnesty" for all Poles in Prisoner of War Camps, NKVD prisons and in Soviet Exile and agreed to a Polish army being formed in the USSR; all those who heard of "the amnesty", and who were able to undertake the journey, set out for the recruitment centres. In 1942 the Polish army and its dependents left the Soviet Union for Persia (today's Iran) to be re-equipped and made ready for battle. Together with units already in England (Polish Navy, Air Force and Army evacuated from France) the Polish Armed Forces in Exile thus became the third largest fighting force in the West after Britain and America. Their Battle Honours include Narvik, the Battle of Britain, Battle of the Atlantic, Tobruk, Monte Cassino, Normandy and Arnhem.

Civilians who escaped from the Soviet Union with the troops were placed in camps in British colonies in India and Africa to await the end of the war and return to their homes in an independent Poland.

Unfortunately, the political settlement between Roosevelt, Stalin and Churchill meant that when the war ended the Soviets annexed Eastern Poland and incorporated it into the Soviet Union, while the rest of Poland became a puppet state with a communist government imposed by Russia. The vast ma-

General K. Sosnkowski reporting to King George VI

jority of Poles rejected this settlement and chose to remain in The West where they could continue the political struggle for an independent Poland while maintaining their language, culture and traditions for an eventual return to their homeland.

When, in July 1945, the British government withdrew recognition from the Polish Government in London, recognised the Warsaw regime imposed by Russia and refused Polish forces a place in the Victory parade, it found itself with a very tricky problem. What to do with a large allied army, air force and navy owing its allegiance to, and under the control of, a government no longer recognised by the British and actively hostile to the government now proclaimed by Britain and the USA as the legitimate government of Poland?

3

One of the options was to repatriate forcibly the Polish armed forces and their dependents to Poland but, as it is succinctly put in a cabinet briefing paper '....it needs to be born in mind that the Polish army is currently the largest fighting force in Italy.' The problem was solved in a pragmatic and very British way. A Polish Resettlement Corps (PRC) was raised as a corps of the British Army and all those wishing to remain in the West were recruited into this newly created corps for the period of their resettlement and demobilisation. Some 125,000 chose to join the PRC and remain in Britain. They were joined by their families and dependents from wherever the fortunes of war had left them, swelling the numbers to well over 200,000. By far the largest number of dependents were those who, having escaped from Siberia with the Polish Army in 1942, had spent the war in Displaced Persons camps in British colonies and protectorates, mainly in India and East Africa. The only way such numbers of men and their families could be accommodated in a war-ravaged Britain was by placing them in camps recently vacated by the Americans and Canadians. There were many such camps in the UK, most were built in the early 1940s in rural areas, often in the grounds of large country estates as Military Hospitals, Army Bases and Airfields. Blackshaw Moor became one of them.

Polish soldiers from the 2nd Corps (now in the PRC) on the road by the Three Horse Shoes Inn

Blackshaw Moor Polish Camp 1946

In 1942/3 at Blackshaw Moor along the A53 Leek to Buxton road, four adjoining army camps were built as part of the war effort. These camps were occupied by the 565th US Anti Aircraft Battalion and also used as transit camps for US troops arriving in the U.K. in preparation for D-day.

With the end of hostilities the Americans vacated the camps and, in 1946, Polish troops returning from Italy and other battlefields of Europe moved into the empty barracks. The abandoned camp became home to men and women from the Polish 2nd Corps who served in the Allied Armed Forces under British command and who, because of the political situation, could not return to their homeland.

Polish soldier Wojciech Iciek with Stanisław and Jan Kapusta

A group of Polish soldiers from the 2nd Corps in Blackshaw Moor - Winter 1947

Map showing Blackshaw Moor's four camps.

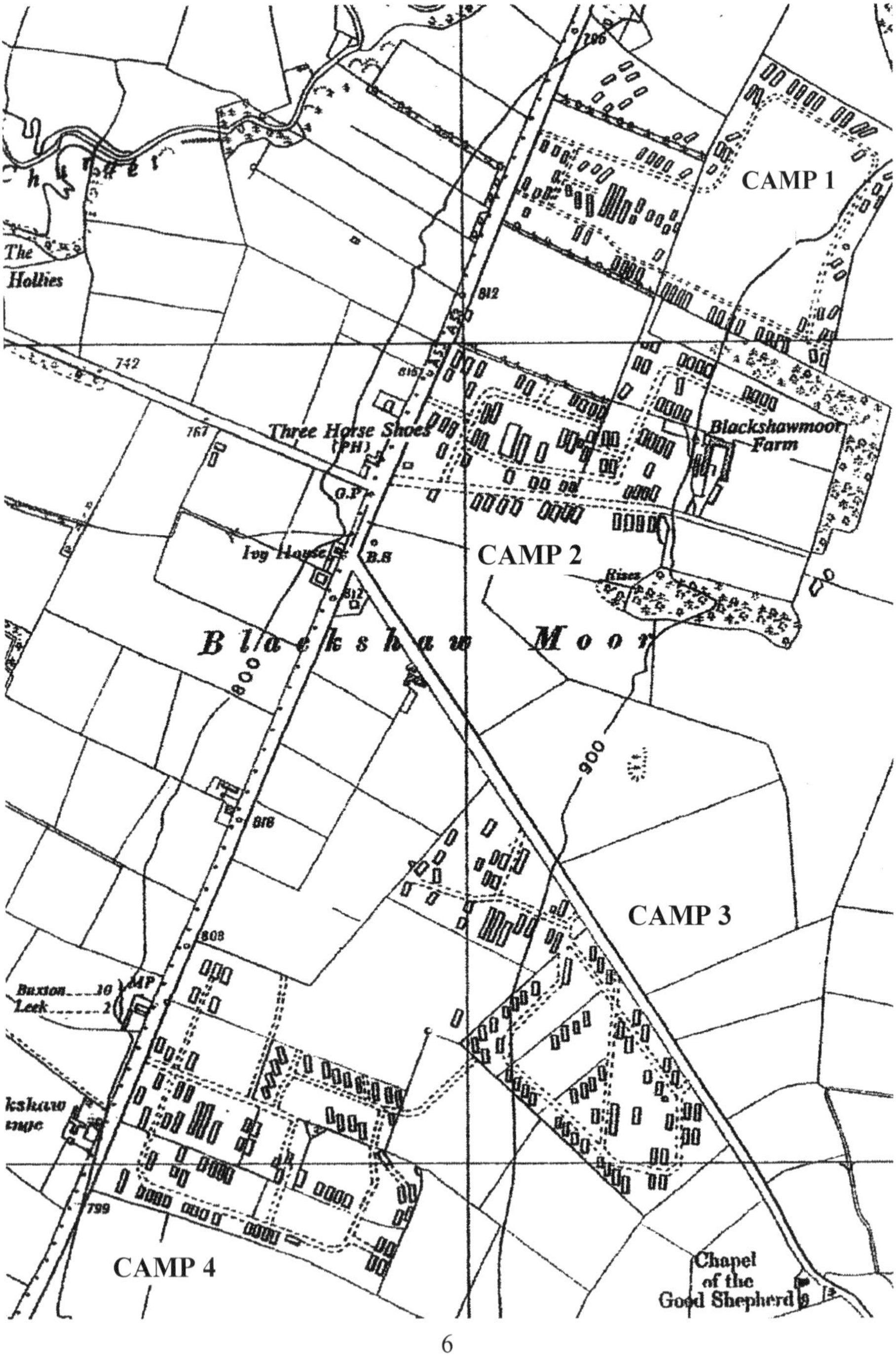

CAMP 1

The Hollies

812

742

767

Three Horse Shoes (PH)

O.P.

Blackshawmoor Farm

Ivy House   B.S

CAMP 2

Rises

B l a c k s h a w   M o o r

800

818

900

CAMP 3

808

Buxton   10
Leek   2

MP

kshaw
nage

799

CAMP 4

Chapel
of the
Good Shepherd

The map shows the layout of the four camps. Camps 1 and 2 were some distance away from camps 3 and 4. In 1946 Polish units of the PRC moved into camps 1 and 4 for the period of time until their demobilisation. Camp 4 became the administration centre and was vacated in late 1948 to make way for an MOD Anzio army training camp. Camp 2 which stood opposite the Three Horse Shoes Inn was handed over by the MOD to the National Service Hostels Corporation (NSHC) for a period of two years to house single Polish men employed in the Buxton Quarries. Camp 3 became married quarters with some families overflowing into the other camps.

Polish and foreign workers in Buxton Quarries 1948

There were approximately 75 huts of various sizes on each site. The huts were divided with studded walls giving each family separate accommodation amounting to one medium sized room, in which the family lived and slept. The families were provided with bedding, furniture and other equipment, just bare necessities, by the Military. A weekly rent of 10 shillings for a husband, 6 sh. for a wife and 3 sh. for each child was collected by the warrant officer on behalf of the Assistance Board. These payments covered rental of furniture, equipment, light and fuel. The huts were heated by a round coke burning pot bellied stove, totally useless for any serious cooking.

Cement works where some of the Blackshaw Moor Poles worked

Each site had a number of communal ablution blocks with showers and toilets, where hot water was available once a week. Water for drinking and cooking had to be carried in buckets from outside stand pipes.

Living in these conditions, especially with young children was extremely difficult. The army had no experience of running civilian camps so the National Assistance Board, which was responsible for other Polish resettlement camps in the UK, approached the NSHC to take over the running of the Blackshaw Moor camps on their behalf but they declined because of the poor state of the huts. In fact, there was some confusion as to who was responsible for what: The MOD looked after the men in uniform until their demobilisation; the NSHC after the single civilian workers employed in local industry; no one took responsibility for the families. This meant that the huts in which the families were living, which were already in a poor state, deteriorated quite badly. Things came to a head in 1948 when the PRC was wound up and the MOD and NSHC vacated the camps, leaving Polish families to fend for themselves, with little or no English language skills and no knowledge of whom to approach for help. Luckily there were a number of English wives of Polish ex-soldiers living in the same appalling conditions. Led by Mrs. Tryerstowski they appealed to the Local Authority which eventually and reluctantly accepted responsibility for Camps 1 and 2. The Ministry of Works were then set to work on converting the huts into dwellings of 2 and 3 bedrooms and kitchen complete with a coal fired cooking range. Water still had to be carried to the huts from the communal stand pipes and the ablution blocks still had to be shared. The work was completed by 1951, greatly improving the conditions of the inhabitants.

A view of the Roaches, from the camp

The Poles in turn set to work on rebuilding their lives and their community, firmly grounded in their faith and cultural traditions. Camp One became the heart of this community. It included a nursery, school, shop, club house and, most importantly, a church. The church and clubhouse were housed in two large corrugated metal Nissen huts in the centre of the camp and most of the camp's social activities revolved around them. The Caravan Club is located on what was Camp One and it is here, around the perimeter of the caravan site, that you can still find some of the derelict huts that were once home to Polish families.

Most Poles are devout Roman Catholics and it is their faith that helped them to survive the war, exile and years in the wilderness. They came to the camps as total strangers from every part of Poland and from all walks of life.

What remains of some of the camps' huts around the perimeter of the Caravan Club site

Doctors, lawyers, teachers, university lectures and aristocrats mixed with farmers, factory workers and simple country folk. This diverse mix of people had to build a new way of life and forge a coherent community in a new country. Every camp became a Little Poland in the middle of the English countryside, clinging to their traditions, culture, language and history. In most camps there was also a Polish priest looking after the spiritual needs of the community.

Keeping Their Faith and Traditions

The Polish Catholic Church has many deep rooted traditions which had become not only religious but also social and cultural celebrations. They were practised with vigour and dedication, playing a large part in the life of the Polish people in Blackshaw Moor. With their priest, Fr. Paweł Sargiewicz, at the helm the first thing the community did was to convert one of the large black corrugated

Nissen huts into a place of worship where Sunday masses, daily services, christenings, funerals and religious festivals were celebrated. All marriages took place in St. Mary's Catholic Church in Leek.

Fr. Paweł Sargiewicz, like many Polish priests during WW2, was imprisoned by the soviets and deported to Siberia. In 1942, after Russia found itself part of the anti Hitler alliance, he joined General Anders' 2nd Corps and became army Chaplain to the troops. He took part in the Italian campaign and was at Monte Cassino; his war effort was recognised both by the church and the army, bestowing on him honours and medals. He came to Blackshaw Moor camp in 1946 with the Polish 2nd Corps from Italy and here he stayed taking on the role of Polish Parish Priest for the families living in the camp and surrounding area, reaching as far as Newcastle and Stoke on Trent. He was much loved by his parishioners and, having gone through the same hell, he understood

Krysia Hermit
In front of the Nissen hut Church distinguished by a timber bell tower and cross (just out of the picture).

their fears and anxieties. Fr Sargiewicz died on 1ˢᵗ September 1967 in a car accident by the Three Horse Shoes Inn.

We all celebrate Christmas and Easter but one of the most colourful and most photographed events in all Polish camps was the Corpus Christi Procession which falls sixty days after Easter, between late May and the middle of June.

Some of the Polish families in front of two large Nissen huts one of which served as a church. In the background is a view of the Roaches.

Each year, regardless of the weather, a procession celebrating Corpus Christi created a buzz and excitement in the camps. From early morning teams of men and women built four altars at strategic points around the camp representing the four evangelists and decorated them with greenery and flowers. After Holy Mass the faithful, in their Sunday best, processed in prayer and song following the priest carrying the Holy Host around the camp to the four altars. Banners and flags representing the various religious and social organisations active in the camp were carried by leading members of the organisations and young people in national costumes. Little girls dressed in white, helped by their mothers, scattered a carpet of flowers as the procession wound its way around the camp.

Fr. Sargiewicz leading a Corpus Christi Procession past the Nissen hut Church.

The Procession making its way through the camp with some of the huts in the background.

Girls in National dress processing with a picture of the Black Madonna are;-
Teresa Krzywicka, Danuta Hryciuk and Krystyna Hermit - 1963

Some of the youngest parishioners with their offering

First Communion

Another annual event which brought the community together was the first Holy Communion of the eight and nine year old children.

Children after their First Communion outside the Nissen hut Church - 1954

Christening

Many christenings took place in the camp's Church.

Christening of twins Danuta and Genowefa Kapusta with godparents Mr. Żurek. Mrs. and Mr. Dziurdzik and Mrs. Kwartnik - 1952

One of the first babies to be born in the camp was Zbyszek Hryciuk. His parents came to Blackshaw Moor as part of the Resettlement Corps in the later part of 1946 from Southern Italy and were met by cold and wet October weather. Their first home was in Camp Four but soon they moved to Camp One. The winter snow came early in January 1947 and, on cue, Zbyszek's mother Władysława went into labour. A foot of snow had fallen overnight and there was little chance of getting to hospital so Zbyszek was born in the First Aid barrack at Camp One.

Baby Zbyszek with his mother and father still in uniform and older sister Basia who was born in Italy - Christmas 1947.

Over the lifetime of the camp many more babies were born. A nursery/infant school was set up for the very young, which enabled their mothers to go to work in local clothing mills, the silk industry and the advanced dyeing works in Leek. Although there was a bus service from Blackshaw Moor to Leek, never the less, in the early years getting to places of work or to the shops was a problem. Some walked to work, the lucky ones had a bike. In time, bikes were replaced by mopeds and small motor bikes and eventually by cars.

16

Growing up in the camp

When children left the camp's infant school they attended local English schools in Leek some three miles from the camp. They, unlike their parents, very quickly picked up the English language, something that adults, particularly the elderly, found hard going.

As late as the mid 1950s, most Poles believed that their stay in England was just another stop on their way back to their homes in Poland; that soon there would be war against the evil Soviet Empire and they would return to Poland as a liberating army. In this context they saw their main duty as bringing up their children in the Polish spirit. To ensure that the children did not forget their mother tongue a Saturday Polish School was set up in the camp where they learned Polish history, culture and traditions as well as reading and writing in Polish. Great emphasis was placed on involving children in all national cultural activities through taking part in national day celebrations, singing and dancing. Most children had some kind of Polish national costume, usually made for them by their mothers, which was worn on national days, at processions, dance performances and at every opportunity at local village fêtes.

Polish children in National costume parading through the streets of Leek

Zbyszek Hryciuk with his three sisters Danusia, Basia and Halina

Although every Part of Poland has its unique regional costume distinguished by colour schemes and embroidery patterns, there are certain common elements. For girls it consists of a colourful skirt, white blouse, a little piny, a headdress and a black velvet bodice embroidered with beads and sequins, each design being unique. Boys outfits are less flamboyant but still colourful.

Mrs. Krawczyk, with Barbara, Danuta and Halina Hryciuk,
Barbara Szmuniewska, Stasia Świeca and Little Karol Szmuniewski.

Basia Hryciuk and Barbara Szmuniewska

Wojtek and Ryszard
Milaszkiewicz

Growing up in the camp with the freedom of wide open spaces was great fun for the children. With few toys, all sorts of games were dreamed up. Any one in possession of a bicycle had many friends. Sadly not all could afford one but there was always a handy father who could assemble the odd bike from parts salvaged from a tip.

Sylwester Jaworski with a friend on their bikes with a view of the Roaches
The Jaworski family emigrated to the USA in 1959.

Sharing a bike; Zbyszek Hryciuk
Ryszard Krzywicki and Tadek Łazowski.

A bike for a teenager living in the middle of nowhere was a must. Barbara Hryciuk and Tadeusz Łazowski proud owners of their bikes

You can see the camp in the background.

Some of the young people from the camp - 1962/63

Tadeusz Łazowski, Elżbieta Markowska, Ryszard Milaszkiewicz, Barbara Szmuniewska, Wojciech Milaszkiewicz, Barbara Hryciuk, Danuta Markowska, Stasia Świeca, Halina Hryciuk, Danuta Hryciuk, Edward Kopeć, Zbyszek Hryciuk, Teresa Krzywicka.

Sport in the camp

Sport flourished in the camps and the Association of Polish Sports Clubs, formed in 1949/50, served to link isolated Polish communities. Most camps could field teams in table tennis, volley ball and football. Invariably there was a field which could serve as a pitch and was always in use. In Blackshaw Moor a large field situated between Camps One and Two was used to hone football skills.

Trainer and referee Mr. W Dziurdzik refereeing a match watched by fans from the camp. Camp 2 can be seen in the background.

The most prestigious event was the Gen. Anders Cup competition in football. Each year the finalists and their supporters would converge on Cannock where the final was held. In 1952 the Blackshaw Moor camp's team "Biały Orzeł" (White Eagle) won the cup 3:2 against "Syrena" (Mermaid) West Bromwich.

Blackshaw Moor's winning team receiving the Gen. Anders Cup in Cannock

New generation; the "White Eagles" football team - 1959

Stanisław Kapusta, Ryszard Widlewski, Ryszard Bielicki, Jan Dziurdzik, Ryszard Krzywicki, Wojciech Milaszkiewicz and the only English member Ken Mountford

A New Era For The Camp Dwellers

In the early 1960s the lower part of Camp Two, opposite the Three Horse Shoes Inn, was demolished to make room for a new council housing estate for the fifty Polish families still living in substandard barracks in the camps. It took a little time for some of the older people to leave the camp, and a way of life that they had become accustomed to during the war, and move the 200 yards or so to the new estate, but in 1964 all the families moved out of the leaky and bleak huts into the fifty two new dwellings on the Tittesworth Estate.

A view of the Tittesworth Estate with the Roaches in the background

At the same time, one of the old brick washhouses that was still standing at the top of Camp Two was renovated and converted into a new church. In October of that year the church was consecrated by Prelate Bronisław Michalski assisted by Polish priests from other nearby Polish parishes, Manchester, Northwich, Prees Higher Heath, Rochdale and the Polish hospital in Penley. It was estimated that over three hundred Poles from around the area attended the ceremony. It was a memorable occasion recalled by all who attended.

There was fear that the new estate would lead to the break up of the Polish community, but since all the fifty families moved together and with their little church on site serving their spiritual needs, the bonds become even stronger.

Consecration of the new Church on the Tittesworth Estate

The old and the new

Anna Sawko admiring the flowers out side one of the camps huts.

Mr. and Mrs. Hryciuk outside their new council house.
The white building in the background is the new church.

Tittesworth Estate became the new little Poland and, for the first time since the war, Polish families were living in real houses. Although the houses were now completed; the gardens, pavements and paths around them were not and, as the landowner started work on demolishing the old camp, the Poles salvaged as much as they could from their gardens in the old camp. Mainly useful things like paving slabs and also plants to improve their surroundings on the new estate.

Over the years the Polish community on the Tittesworth estate dwindled to just a handful of ageing ex-camp dwellers. In 1993 the little church closed its doors but the building lives on. Today the hut is still there although totally unrecognisable. It started its life as an army washroom, in 1965 was converted into a place of worship and now a lovely stone clad bungalow. The only new addition is a garage.

Nothing lasts for ever, children became adults and left "Little Poland" to find their own way in life. Some into further education and on to universities. Others, in pursuit of better jobs, moved out of the area and a number emigrated to the United States. Still others married childhood friends from the camp setting up homes locally in Leek, Stoke, Newcastle-under-Lyme and the surrounding area.

The houses that were built in 1964 for Polish families, are now homes to British families. There are just two descendants of Polish families who grew up in Blackshaw Moor camp left on the estate. One of them is Witek Hermit and his wife Teresa. Witek, now in his 80s, told me of an incident that he was involved in as a teenager. Whilst playing with a friend around Camp Three they came across an empty hut on the edge of the camp and inside discovered a sack full of grenades. Filling their pockets they went into the field and started throwing them in anticipation of a big explosion, luckily for the boys the grenades were not primed. He said that they were collared by local bobby PC Dawson who strongly reprimanded them. With a chuckle he said "The army bomb disposal unit was called out to deal with the rest of the grenades. Those were the days."

Today nostalgia still draws many back to the place where they were born and grew up. Seeking out what is still left of the camp and reminiscing not only of the hardship their parents had to endure bringing them up in such primitive conditions, but also of the freedom and good times spent there as children in Blackshaw Moor Polish Camp.

The Minorczyk family on one of their nostalgic visits to Camp One standing in what could have been their hut.

Below; the floor slab and rubble that was once a hut.

Blackshaw Moor Caravan Club Site

For many years the site of Camp One was abandoned to the elements. Some of the huts that were still standing were used by the local farmer for animal shelters or to store straw and farm equipment but essentially nature took over.

In 1979 the Caravan Club bought the site, cleared the land and created an attractive, terraced site with 89 spacious and level hard standing pitches. The site became very popular with caravanners who enjoy the beautiful views, walks and fresh air of the Peak District as well as take an interest in the history of the locality they visit.

The wardens, Anthony and Sheila Kendall and Perry and Anne Marie Robbins, were made aware of the history of the site by regular visitors whose families lived in Camp One some seventy years ago. The wardens were so moved by their stories that they contacted Ian Spendlove, their Regional Manager, and suggested that a commemorative plaque be erected drawing visitors' attention to the unusual history of the site and offering them an insight into a short but important period of post war Anglo-Polish history. The memory of the Polish camp at Blackshaw Moor and the sympathy felt towards the Polish community found its expression when Nettlebank Memorials, the stone masons, were approached to do the work and they immediately offered to provide the stone but charge only for the inscription.

Early years of camping on the site.

Blackshaw Moor Caravan Club Site today with the Roaches just visible above the shrubbery and, below, the site office and facilities centre

The commemorative plaque to be unveiled on the 16th of September 2015